Maui Bound

PHOTOGRAPHY BY

HAWAI'I'S FINEST PHOTOGRAPHERS

TEXT BY

TOM STEVENS

EDITED BY

BETTY FULLARD-LEO

DESIGNED BY

DAVID A. OKA

PACIFIC ISLANDS PUBLISHING, LTD.

WAILUKU, MAUI AND HONOLULU, O'AHU

Maui Bound
© 1991 by Pacific Islands Publishing, Ltd. and Ka Lima o Maui

Special acknowledgement is extended to Bishop Museum Press for the Hawaiian proverbs reprinted from the book "Hui No'eau," by Mary Kawena Pukui, 1983.

Page 4, 5 A sliver of sun remains moments before Hawaii's total solar eclipse, July 11, 1991.

First edition, September 1991

ISBN: 0-9630576-0-X

Produced by   and
Pacific Islands Publishing, Ltd.   1109 Bethel Street, Suite 210
P.O. Box 1475   Honolulu, Hawai'i 96813
Kahului, Hawai'i 96732

Printed in Hong Kong

FOREWARD

4

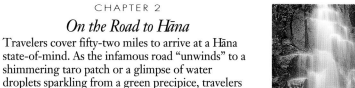

Foreward

'Oi kau ka lā, e hana i ola honua

WHILE THE SUN YET SHINES, DO ALL YOU CAN

When the demigod Māui snagged his fish hook on the ocean floor, was it just a lucky accident that he pulled Polynesia from the sea?

Māui had plenty of luck, good and bad, during his reign as the Pacific's foremost trickster, but legend suggests he did little by accident. There was usually method in his mischief – and a message. To pull Polynesia from the sea required cooperation among Māui's brawny paddlers. All had to *"hoe aku i ka wa'a,"* do their share to paddle their canoes ahead, or the islands would still be miles beneath the ocean.

Cooperation also figures in Māui's greatest Hawaiian feat – the capture and slowing down of the sun. Before Māui cast his net of vines across Mount Haleakalā to snare the awakening sun, that willful orb sped capriciously through the sky, leaving the women too little daylight to dry their *kapa* cloth (made of *wauke* or *māmaki* bark) and the men too little warmth to cure their fish.

"Eh bruddah, slow down and cooperate," Māui ordered. The sun bucked and twisted and roared with outrage, but Māui had woven his net strongly, plaiting many vines into one. At length, the sun complied, and harmony between sky and earth was restored.

For a thousand years, the Māui legends were among the great learning stories of the Pacific. Wherever the Polynesians voyaged, to Tetiaroa, New Zealand, Tonga, Samoa, Fatu Hiva and far Hawai'i, Māui's message was the same: strength and guile are not enough. All paddlers must pull together. Nowhere is this clearer than on the one island among Polynesia's thousands that bears the demigod's name: Maui.

It is not the largest nor most important island in Polynesia, nor is it the most beautiful – Moorea stakes that claim. Māui's beaches are no whiter than a hundred others, its streams no clearer, its bays and valleys no more bountiful. The great volcano Haleakalā, House-of-the-Sun, bows to New Zealand's lofty southern alps and to Hawai'i's mighty Mauna Kea and Mauna Loa. Even Maui's "torso" shape does not distinguish it – Tahiti and Samoa share the same configuration.

Why, then, is Maui special? Why does this island alone bear the Pacific's most famous name? Mauians make Maui special. They came first from Tahiti and the Marquesas, arriving by the seventh or eighth century a.d. Among them were brawny seafarers who could endure weeks of paddling in open canoes, skilled farmers, fishermen and kapa makers who brought everything needed to start life in a new world.

They settled in groups on *ahupua'a*, wedge-shaped land divisions extending from the mountains to the sea, that supplied them with all the necessities: wood for fires and canoes from the uplands, land for taro, coconut and bananas and fish from the ocean. The *ali'i*, high chiefs, and their *kahuna*, priests, were the most powerful beings. *Heiau*, religious temples, were built of stone to honor four gods, Kū, Kane, Lono, and Kanaloa, and countless minor gods who regulated all aspects of daily living through a complex *kapu* or taboo system. Men and women could not eat together, and certain foods such as bananas were forbidden to women, for example.

Other Mauians arrived more than a thousand years later following the charts of British navigator and explorer, Captain James Cook, who first sighted the Hawaiian Islands on January 18, 1778. It wasn't until 1795 that King Kamehameha I unified the Hawaiian Islands, and war among the competing chiefs ended. By 1804, Kamehameha moved his court from Lahaina, shifting much of the importance of trade and policy making to O'ahu. The monarchy was established, but the news of Cook's discovery brought to Maui and the other islands explorers and military delegations, then traders, whalers, merchants seeking sandalwood and missionaries seeking souls to save. The first Maui missionaries reached Lahaina in 1820, right on the heels of the establishment of Lahaina as a riotous whaling port.

From China came tireless workers who would build the island's railroads and irrigation ditches and later raise potatoes to ship to the California gold rush "forty-niners." With the decreasing isolation of the islands and the introduction of new religions, the kapu system was broken, ushering in the way to rapid change.

There followed Mauians from other far-flung locales, many of them islands. From the Azores and Madeiras came Portuguese settlers seeking freedom from poverty, military conscription and grim Atlantic fogs. Seasick new immigrants staggered ashore from Japan, Korea, Okinawa, Puerto Rico and the Philippines after weeks at sea. They came as contract plantation workers, and many stayed when their contracts were fulfilled.

World War II brought thousands of Allied servicemen and women through Maui. Many returned at war's end to settle and seek their fortunes in the islands. Statehood in 1959 and the commercial boom that followed, drew waves of new residents from around the globe: builders, hotel workers, teachers, lawyers, doctors, potentates and pleasure-seekers.

Maui hosts more than two million visitors annually, and some of them become residents as well. But it is not enough simply to choose Maui – Maui also chooses. Ever since its first discoverers paddled ashore more than a thousand years ago, Maui has chosen those who get along with one another. It is no easy process, this getting along. The differences between cultures, ethnic groups and religions are as numerous as summer stars.

Luckily for Maui, the island's founders and most who followed came from societies where cooperation is the highest art form. From the Hawaiians, later Mauians learned the concepts of *aloha*, universal love; *kokua*, survival through sharing; and *mālama āina*, stewardship of the land. And in the close quarters of plantation camps, they learned to respect and appreciate each others' food, games, customs and beliefs.

Nearly all had come from fishing and farming communities where human activity was governed not by clocks, but by the unalterable rhythms of nature. Already attuned to the myriad interrelationships of plants, animals, soil, water and weather, Maui's immigrants soon shared the Hawaiians' nurturing attitude toward the land, sea and sky and all life therein. Not only did this bind them to the living spirit of the land, it bound them to each other.

This is what makes Maui special. Visitors who stay only briefly speak of the island's stunning beauty, mild weather or plush accommodations. Those who stay longer speak about the warmth and goodwill of Maui's people, because the island has always chosen givers over takers, sharers over hoarders, and the kind gesture over the proud boast. Add laughter, music and a love of life, and you have a legacy worthy of a demigod.

Along with many legends, Māui left physical evidence of his greatest feats. After pulling up the islands, for instance, he set his great curved fish hook in the night sky. It still shimmers there as the constellation Scorpio, called throughout Polynesia *Mānai a ka lani*, needle-in-the-sky. Who knows, perhaps Māui had a hand in drawing the moon across the sun to stage the solar eclipse that darkened island skies on July 11, 1991.

Greater still, is the legacy he left in the sparkling sea below. It is an island in mid-Pacific where even the sun must slow down and cooperate. It is the island Maui, where people learned to live with nature and with each other.

From the Mountains

CHAPTER 1

He ʻohu ke aloha; ʻaʻohe kuahiwi kau ʻole

LOVE IS LIKE MIST, THERE IS NO MOUNTAINTOP THAT IT DOES NOT SETTLE UPON

chain of volcanic seamounts sizzled up out of the mid-Pacific during a period of twenty-five million years, slowly creating the Hawaiian archipelago. Maui lies near the southern end of that diagonal 1,500-mile mountain range.

Each seamount formed as a "weak spot" in a slowly moving tectonic plate on Earth's crust allowed spurts of molten lava to ooze upward, finally spewing out onto the ocean floor. New lava covered old, century after century, forming an undersea mountain at each geologic "hot spot." As the plate inched off toward the northwest, new seamounts formed at the hot spot, and older ones were carried slowly away like knobs on a crocodile's back.

Not all seamounts grew large enough to reach the ocean's surface, but 124 did. These include the eight major islands at the southern end of the chain, the group known as Hawaiʻi, as well as the remote northerly atolls Midway and Kure and storm-lashed crags like Necker, Nihoa and the French Frigate Shoals.

Many of these islands, now just slivers of reef and rock, were once towering mountains like Oʻahu's 4,000-foot Mount Kaʻala, Molokaʻi's mile-high Puʻu o Hoku, Maui's 10,000-foot Haleakalā, and the Big Island's twin titans, 13,000-foot Mauna Loa and Mauna Kea.

Once they moved off the hot spot and stopped growing, these older islands subsided into the sea, abraded to mere nubs by the erosive power of sun, wind and waves. A similar fate awaits Maui in a few million years as well.

While Maui rests on two volcanic columns – mile-high Puʻukukui (West Maui) and its two-mile-high brother, Haleakalā (East Maui) – the island once boasted five major volcanoes and a landed area nearly as vast as the Big Island. During the Ice Age, geologists speculate, the world's sea levels were so much lower than they are today that Maui, Kahoʻolawe, Lānaʻi and Molokaʻi were all part of a single land mass. When the ice caps melted, the rising ocean flooded this mega-Maui's low-lying plains, creating the four neighbor islands we know today.

As the older of the two sibling volcanoes, Puʻukukui (candlenut hill) shows the ravages of time more dramatically than does youthful Haleakalā. Its crater and walls are so severely eroded that Puʻukukui is scarcely recognizable as a single peak. Viewing the worn volcano's skyline, it is no surprise that most residents call this area the "West Maui Mountains."

While the West Maui volcano has lost much to erosion, it has gained much as well. Few places in the Pacific boast such breathtaking valleys and sheer escarpments as those visible from ʻĪao on a clear day. Thousands of years of rainfall have carved ravines, canyons and cataracts as dramatic as any in the American west. Stream-fed ʻĪao Valley, in fact, has been called "the Yosemite of the Pacific."

If ʻĪao is home to Maui's Yosemite, then Haleakalā must be compared to some other-worldly planet. But nature's handiwork remains spectacular. Dropping more than 3,000 feet in ten miles, the crater is ringed by crumbling canyon walls, plateaus and mesas straight out of the old west. Cactus-like silversword plants reinforce this image.

Other worlds coexist here, too. The upper rim is moon-like; a cratered, arid dome studded with cinder cones of red, black, gold and gray, some 500 feet high. So unearthly is this basalt-bombed no-man's land that it served as a rehearsal stage for the Apollo astronauts.

As the crater descends into the moist, rolling clouds of Maui's eastern end, a strange thing happens. The silent moonscape of the summit gives way to a foggy rain forest alive with the songs of some of Hawaiʻi's few remaining native birds. Thick meadow grass pastures park rangers' horses, and the water catchment tanks are rarely empty.

While hardy souls hike through the crater or overnight at its cabins and camp grounds, most visitors are content to savor spectacular sunrise and sunset vistas from the crater rim. The two-mile altitude that furnishes some of the clearest night viewing on Earth for astronomers at nearby "Science City," (where much of the research for President Reagan's Star Wars program takes place), also creates astounding cloudscapes and light shows at dawn and dusk.

Descending through belts of fog and patches of misty sunlight, returning motorists enjoy Haleakalā's more domesticated side: a picturesque patchwork quilt of cattle ranches, flower farms, orchards, gardens and villages.

Cycling enthusiasts throng the roadsides, where they battle twenty-knot crosswinds and speeding drivers while training for the annual "Cycle to the Sun" race. This thirty-mile, uphill grind from Pāʻia to the Haleakalā summit mirrors its predecessor, a footrace called "Run to the Sun." The grueling event was born when three Maui runners dared themselves to make the 10,000-foot ascent, then couldn't back out.

Cloaking Haleakalā's southern flank in a mantle of emerald green are the high pastures and softly rolling meadows of ʻUlupalakua Ranch. Established by King Kamehameha III during the 1840s, the original tract of several thousand acres was leased for sugar cultivation and milling until purchased by the sea captain James Makee in 1856. Named "Rose Ranch" for his wife's favorite hobby, Makee's new homestead became a country retreat for guests as eminent as King David Kalākaua and the American literary giant Robert Louis Stevenson.

ʻUlupalakua's prominence devolved in part from its proximity to the boat landing at Mākena a few miles downslope. Cattle were driven to Mākena, then "swum" offshore to waiting vessels. Similarly, provisions bound for Upcountry communities often came ashore at Mākena when high seas or foul weather closed Maui's windward anchorages. Illicit opium shipments bound for the Chinese community at Kēōkea also traversed the Mākena to ʻUlupalakua route.

In 1963, present owner C. Pardee Erdman bought the historic ranch. He diversified ranch operations to include sheep raising and cultivation of wine grapes. Erdman and Napa, California vintner Emil Tedeschi founded Hawaiʻi's only commercial winery at ʻUlupalakua in 1974. Current production includes pineapple wines as well as award-winning rosé, Beaujolais and champagne from carnelian grapes.

Near ʻUlupalakua and below the dense, fog-shrouded Polipoli forest is the hamlet of Kēōkea, once a thriving Chinese farming community, later an employee town for the handsome Kula Hospital nearby. In its mid-nineteenth-century heyday, Kēōkea residents did a brisk business as purveyors of fruit, vegetables and even clean laundry to thousands of fortune-seekers then pouring into the mining camps and boom towns of gold rush-era California. In the early years of this century, Kēōkea sheltered Sun Yat Sen, the philosophical and spiritual father of modern China, and members of his exiled family.

To the east of Kēōkea lie the Upcountry towns of Waiakoa, called Kula, Pūlehu, Ōmaʻopio, Pukalani, Hāliʻimaile, Makawao and Olinda. These settlements, some historic, some youthful, like twenty-year-old Pukalani, are favored homesites for Mauians willing to swap an increasingly stressful commute for the clean air, rural surroundings and small-town friendliness of the area sometimes called "cloud country."

While most Upcountry residents commute to jobs in central Maui or the resort areas, others work the rich, powdery soil of Kula and Ōma'opio. Predominant crops include sweet Maui onions, Kula potatoes, carnations, cabbage and lettuce, greenhouse ornamentals, artichokes – and many showy varieties of protea flowers introduced to Kula in the 1970s from their native Australia and South Africa.

Surrounding this necklace of Upcountry towns are the magnificent pasture lands and windbreak forests of 30,000-acre Haleakalā Ranch and its smaller neighbors, Kā'anolu and Erehwon ("nowhere" spelled backward). Before paved roads reached the area, cattle from these ranches were driven overland, directly downhill to Kahului for shipment.

While the upper reaches of the ranches extend to the crater rim, Haleakalā's seaward slopes are a vast, wind-rippled carpet of sugar cane dotted here and there by silvery *pūnāwai*, irrigation ponds. A green-gray belt of pineapple runs from Pukalani to Makawao, centering in the Maui Land and Pineapple Company's Hāli'imaile baseyard.

Just upslope is the picturesque former cowboy town of Makawao, now a fast-growing residential community and tourist stop. While occasional residents still ride their horses along Baldwin or Makawao Avenues, the town has become increasingly gentrified as hitching rails give way to galleries, clothing boutiques, lively restaurants and night clubs, making the town a magnet for Upcountry singles and Maui's burgeoning European and windsurfer contingents.

But while Makawao and other Upcountry towns are not as rural as they once were, the changes have been evolutionary rather than revolutionary. Due in part to a long-term building moratorium mandated by the area's rickety water system, in part to concerned stewardship from landowners and leaseholders, Upcountry is still low rise and low key. Longtime landmarks like Kēōkea's Fong Store and Kula Hospital, Holy Ghost Church, Urudomo onion farm and Kula Lodge, Calasa Service, the Pukalani Superette, and Haleakala Dairy, St. Joseph's Church, Kitada's and Komoda Store remain cherished elements of the community.

Horsey Olinda and the rainy, guava-scented pastures of Ha'ikū form Upcountry's eastern fence line. Beyond lies the vast upland rain forest from which Maui draws most of its water; below, weaving and cornering like a mongoose on the run, is the fabled Hāna Road.

Pages 8, 9 – Haleakalā Crater
Sunrises on Haleakalā are so spectacular, they attract
pre-dawn visitors all the way from West Maui resorts.

Above – Haleakalā Crater
Hikers, who descend Sliding Sands Trail into
Haleakalā Crater, often exit the crater via the
Halemau'u Trail, popularly dubbed the
"Switchback."

Left – Haleakalā Crater
Often cloaked in clouds at 10,000 feet, Haleakalā's
crater resembles a multicolored moonscape, while its
outer slopes are lush, rolling ranch lands.

Above – Haleakalā National Park
Hawai'i's state bird, the nēnē, is thought to be a descendent of the Canadian goose, uniquely adapted to its mountain environment.

Right – Haleakalā Crater
An endangered species, the iridescent silversword plant dies once it has finished blooming.

Above left – Haleakalā
The slopes of Haleakalā provide ideal conditions for
aerial adventurers.

Above right – Mount Haleakalā
A mountain biker braves the rough terrain on the
slopes of Haleakalā.

Left – Haleakalā Crater
Rare snowfalls on Haleakalā furnish barely enough
snow for winter play.

Above – Kula
A flower farmer tends her carnations in the cool
Upcountry air.

Right – Kula
The King protea is the showiest of protea varieties.

Far right – Kula
Protea (the pincushion is shown here) were success-
fully introduced as an income-producing crop for
Upcountry growers.

Facing Page – Kula
Early morning mist often blankets the rolling hills in
the Kula district.

Above left – Kula
Masa Uradomo's forty-plus acre farm in Kula yields cabbages, as well as onions, lettuce, romaine and daikon.

Above right – 'Ulupalakua
Award-winning wines from carnelian grapes are produced at Tedeschi Vineyards.

Left – 'Ulupalakua
Historic 'Ulupalakua Ranch today is a 25,000-acre working cattle and sheep ranch.

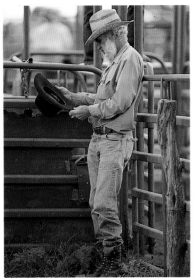

Above left – Makawao
A seasoned cowboy waits for the rodeo to begin.

Above right – Kaupō
As in early Hawai'i, roundups are an annual event on
Maui's vast ranches.

Right – Makawao
A paniolo (Hawaiian cowboy) gives the shaka sign in
a good-natured greeting.

Far left – Upcountry
Smoke sizzles from hot branding irons, as paniolos brand young cattle after the roundup.

Left – Makawao
This *keiki*, child, seems destined to grow up to be a cowboy.

Facing page – Makawao
It's "Ride 'em cowboy," while a rodeo clown waits to divert the bull after the rider has been thrown.

Above – Makawao
Double roping is a fast-moving rodeo event for all concerned.

Left – Makawao
Every second counts in this "mug and steer" contest.

Above left – Kula
Far below, house lights twinkle on in Wailuku and
Kahului as the sun sets along the Haleakalā Highway.

Above right– Makawao
An old-fashioned barber's pole still marks the Aloha
Barber Shop, in business since 1910.

Right – Kula
Kamaʻāina Peter Baldwin and his wife, Gini , enjoy
a country life style in Kula.

Facing page – Makawao
Once a vital hub for Upcountry cowboys and other
residents, Makawao has become a tourist attraction
with galleries, restaurants and night clubs.

CHAPTER 2

On the Road to Hāna

Pō na maka i ka noe, i ka pahululu i ke ala loa

THE EYES ARE BLINDED BY THE MIST THAT HAUNTS THE LONG TRAIL

Rising and plunging sedately like a roller coaster on Hawaiian time, the Hāna Road leads white-knuckled motorists through 600 turns and across fifty-four narrow bridges, some of them nearly a century old. This is not a journey for the faint of heart, nor for those in a hurry.

"Hawaiian time" is a consideration on the Hāna Road, because Hāna is a Hawaiian place. The whole idea of going to Hāna is to be slowed down so much by the time you arrive that all your senses are open to the area's extraordinary peace and beauty. The Hāna Road handles this assignment admirably – countless hairpin turns and sudden glimpses over 500-foot ocean cliffs throttle back even the most assertive drivers. In other words, you'll get there when you get there. What's the rush?

Of course, the whole idea of "getting there" may be misleading, since Hāna is as much a state of mind as a destination. It is the soul of what remains Hawaiian in a modern Hawai'i: a spiritual and cultural resource that longtime islanders revere as *pōhaku*, the rock. For Hawaiians from other parts of the state, a visit to Hāna has elements of a pilgrimage.

And so it should. This coast is one of the most venerable and venerated, continuously settled places in Hawai'i, with habitation established for more than a thousand years. Regional place names like Hāmoa (Samoa) and Kahikinui (Great Tahiti) indicate that the Hāna Coast was as important to its discoverers as it remains to their descendants. This is not just a place to see; it is a way to feel.

Of course, what many travelers feel when they finally reach Hāna is relief. "I survived the road to Hāna!" is the joking quip on commemorative T-shirts sold at the final destination. For those accustomed to traveling fifty miles in forty minutes on a turnpike, the Hāna Road can be a survival test. If they buy the T-shirt, at least their senses of humor will have survived.

More important may be one's sense of wonder, for the Hāna Road is an engineering marvel of the Pacific. Just to see the rugged coastline from land is remarkable; to travel through it smoothly and safely (if slowly) is truly wondrous. A fifty-two-mile ribbon of asphalt clinging to treacherous cliffs and then snaking inland to cross jungled ridges and ravines, Hāna Road rewards its travelers richly, filling the senses at every turn.

From Pā'ia, once Maui's largest plantation town, to the gradually lumbering sea cliffs at Ho'okipa, the view is green and blue: sugar cane on one side, ocean on the other. The northeasterly trade winds that sweep down this coast toward Kahului bring out the silver in flickering cane leaves and crown East Maui's peacock-blue waters with dazzling crests of spray.

Hāna Highway landmarks, like the old Kaunoa School in Spreckelsville, pavilioned H. P. Baldwin Beach Park, Pā'ia's stately Rinzai-zen and Mantokuji Buddhist temples, and Mama's Fish House restaurant at Kū'au add scenic variety, as do the hundreds of neon-bright windsurf sails visible on any blustery afternoon. A summer-long series of team slalom windsurfing competitions are held in the fierce winds that buffet East Maui's Kanahā-to-Ho'okipa coastline, a waterway that is to windsurfing as Newport is to sailing or Everest to mountaineering. Each spring and fall, when huge north swells combine with steady winds, the world's top windsurfers gather at Ho'okipa to astonish onlookers with loop-the-loops and high speed runs across monster waves. In addition to attracting windsurfers, Ho'okipa Beach Park, a crescent of coarse yellow sand hugging reddish cliffs, is a fine place to appreciate the ancient Hawaiian sport of surfing.

After Ho'okipa and the hidden rodeo arena at the mouth of a vast fissure called Māliko Gulch, Hāna Highway climbs and descends ever loftier ridges as the coastline steepens. The land becomes greener and wetter, the sea darker. The sweet scents of white and yellow ginger, strawberry guavas and eucalyptus fill the cool air. Waterfalls tumble into dark, icy pools beside the road, beckoning travelers to stop for a chilly dip. Those who stop may see daring island youths leaping from forty-foot ledges into pools that at times seem little wider than bathtubs.

Also tempting travelers to pull over for a scenic pause are the taro-farming villages of Ke'anae and Wailua, each claiming churches more than a century old and picturesque country houses surrounded by some of Hawai'i's most beautifully groomed lawns. Plants of a thousand varieties grow in lush profusion at such Hāna roadside nurseries as the Ke'anae Arboretum, Ali'i and Helani Gardens and Hāna Gardenland.

Past the wide mouth of Honomanū Bay, a surfer's winter season favorite, past the one-time rubber plantation town of Nāhiku and its rough-water boat landing, the road at last begins its descent into Hāna. Landmarks here include the 500-year-old Pi'ilanihale Heiau, the largest temple in the state and Maui's best preserved pre-Cook structure; the Blue Pool in its ethereal beauty; and the startling black sand beaches and submarine caves at Wai'ānapanapa State Park.

Hāna's story could fill a book – and has. Its history – from Polynesian settlement through fierce interisland battles, from rowdy whalers and circuit-riding missionaries to sugar cane plantations, ranching and tourism – is the equal of any in Hawai'i.

The demigod Māui stood atop Hāna's Ka'uiki Head to push the sky high enough so that the first humans could walk erect. In a cave at the base of the same monolith, Ka'ahumanu, the spirited revolutionary who would become Maui's most prominent convert to Christianity and Kamehameha the Great's most powerful queen, was born. Hāna was also the site of pivotal land and sea engagements over the centuries, the latest being Maui King Kahekili's bloody but indecisive campaign against the young Kamehameha in the 1780s.

Beyond Ka'uiki, the velvet pastures of Hāna Ranch tumble from moist, watercolor skies to the cream-flecked cobalt of Hāna's dancing waves. Those game enough to drive on past the varicolored beaches (black Wai'ānapanapa, brown Hāna Bay, red Kaihalulu and golden Koki and Hāmoa) will view some of Hawai'i's most scenic estates and contented cows along the rugged Kīpahulu Coast.

Kīpahulu is the site of the famous Seven Pools at 'Ohe'o, a natural wonder saved from resort development through the foresight of the Sierra Club, The Nature Conservancy and financier Laurence Rockefeller. Another famous American name now synonymous with Kīpahulu is that of Charles Lindbergh, the "Lone Eagle" aviator buried here in 1974.

Next, ruggedly scenic Kaupō Ranch, whose upper pastures meet the eastern fence lines of Haleakalā National Park, spreads across the mountain. The tiny cowboy community of Kaupō includes 150-year-old Catholic and Protestant churches and wood-planked Kaupō Store, where electricity first reached the Hāna Coast through the efforts of former proprietor Nick Soon.

Beyond Kaupō lies a road so tortuous and brutal, so frequently washed out and so scarcely paved, that it makes Hāna Road seem like the Autobahn.

Page 26, 27 – Pā'ia
Pā'ia Town is the last stop for food and gas before embarking on the scenic, fifty-mile road to Hāna.

Above – Kanahā Beach Park
All summer long, windsurfers compete in team slalom races.

Right - Ho'okipa Beach Park
Hawai'i's own windsurfing champion, Robbie Naish prepares for a day of skimming the waves.

Facing Page – Ho'okipa
A windsurfer goes airborne at Ho'okipa, Hawai'i's most famous windsurfing beach.

Above – Keʻanae
Wetland taro flourishes in a patchwork of plots on the remote Keʻanae Peninsula.

Right – Keʻanae
Taro was a nutritious staple for early Hawaiians, who brought seedlings with them when they sailed to their new homeland in ancient times.

Facing Page – Wailua
A farmer lines up a parallel row in preparation for setting out new taro plants.

Above left – Hāna
The bark of the rainbow eucalyptus sports an
intriguing pattern of colors.

Above – Hāna Highway
Bicyclists enjoy the challenges of Hāna Highway's
many curves and hills, as well as spectacular scenery
along the way.

Right – Hāna Highway
A lau hala weaver demonstrates the technique of
creating bowls from the green pandanus leaf.

Facing page – Hāna Highway
The pristine beauty of Twin Falls can be enjoyed by
anyone willing to make a quarter-mile hike off the
highway.

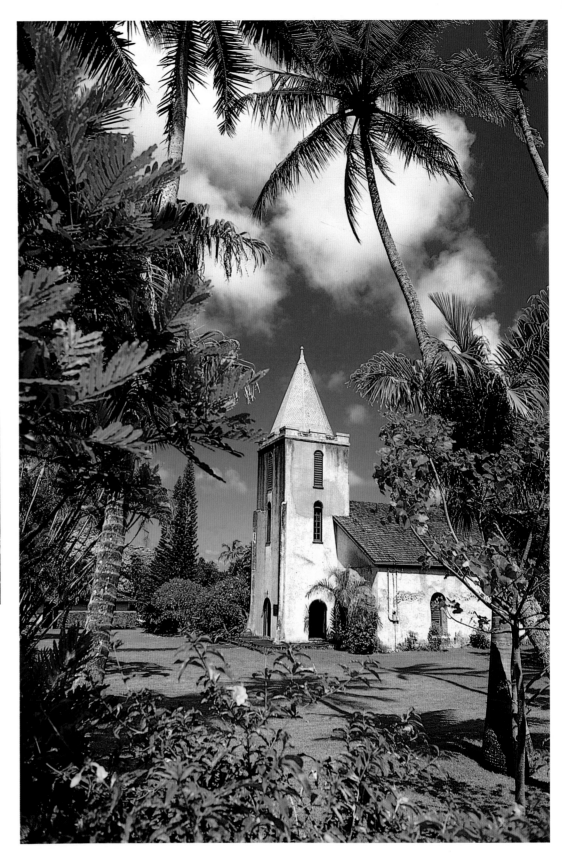

Page 36 – Keʻanae Peninsula
Lava formations bathed in sea mist have an ethereal quality.

Page 37 – Hāna
The sun rises over ʻAlau Island from Koki Beach.

Above – Kīpahulu
A lei on Charles Lindbergh's gravesite imparts a quiet reverence in peaceful surroundings.

Right – Hāna
Wānanalua Congregational Church is an important social element of community life in Hāna.

Left – Hāna
Tiny Malaikini is perhaps Hāna's best known
ambassador of aloha.

Above – Hāna
Youngsters of all ages and sizes participate in spirited
soccer competition.

Above right – Hāna
The regulars at Tutu's Snack Shop "talk story" on a
lazy afternoon.

Facing page – Hāna Highway
Waterfalls are too numerous to name along the road to Hāna.

Above – Kīpahulu
The pools at ʻOheʻo Gulch offer placid waters for swimmers brave enough to take a chilly dip.

Left – Kīpahulu
Fresh flowers and foliage are placed by anonymous residents regularly at this roadside shrine along the highway.

CHAPTER 3

Maui Style

E lei kau, e lei hoʻoilo i ke aloha

LOVE IS WORN LIKE A WREATH THROUGH THE SUMMERS AND THE WINTERS

On a windy Friday afternoon one November, a lone Maui man swung a sledgehammer at a sturdy wedge-shaped block of wood. With each grunting blow, the half-ton cook stove resting atop the block rose a fraction of an inch. When the first wedge had been driven to its hilt, a second was pounded in beneath it.

Corner by corner, wedge upon wedge, the huge cast iron stove inched upward through the afternoon. Finally, just before nightfall, it reached the desired height for that weekend's task: the preparation of a lūʻau for 2,000 friends and family members.

After ensuring that the stove was waist high and level all around, the hammerer set his sledge aside and untied the T-shirt bandana from his wrinkled forehead.

"Good enough," he pronounced, then strolled off toward the lūʻau tents to help his granddaughter string lights, snapping the T-shirt playfully as he went.

Because he had been the only one available in Kahakuloa village that day to raise the stove, the hammerer chose a time-tested method: a sledge and a pile of wedge blocks. When a lūʻau guest complimented him later on his solo feat, the man looked at the ground and shrugged shyly.

"We no work fast here," he grinned, "but we work smart."

It was a Maui-style situation: hard work approached creatively, carried out cheerfully, acknowledged without boastfulness. And the party that followed went on for three days.

What is it about Maui? This island has been hyped so successfully in recent years, packaged and sold so often, that sometimes it's hard to remember there really is a steak under all that sizzle.

Yet long before Maui became a household word, before the rock stars and Lear jets and celebrity golf and tennis tournaments, this island had something special, something that continues to set it apart through all the splash and dazzle.

Call it Maui style.

It is a combination of heritage, hard work and sly good humor. There is no vanity in it. When Mauians call their island "*nō ka ʻoi,*" the best, it is with dignity and quiet pride, not the "come on down and deal" hysteria of some late-night T.V. car salesman. When Mauians greet each other, they do so with the respect and warmth of long association. Loyalties run generations deep here, as does a legacy of tolerance and cooperation forged amid the hardships of plantation life.

Maui style means taking important things seriously – family, friendship, food, livelihood – and letting other things go. Maui people are good at letting things go. All who came to the island originally, and many who come today, sold all they owned, bade farewell to their homelands and the past and took a bold leap into the unknown.

Whether they were Polynesians driven into exile by more powerful chiefs, immigrant laborers staking everything on a dangerous job in a faraway place, or earnest young seekers arriving by one-way ticket with $50 to spare, all had this in common: they did not fear change.

Acceptance of change is a requisite for living happily on Maui, where entire communities have risen, flourished and been bulldozed to rubble in the course of a lifetime. Many of those born here have seen their birth places, grammar schools and villages vanish into green seas of sugar cane or spiky gray phalanxes of pine. They have watched deserts become cities and remote camping spots become world-class resorts. Accept change? Mauians thrive on change.

Maui style means being interested in the new. When some new fad or fashion hits the island, for instance, Maui youngsters jump into it like bare feet into Flo-Jos. Are four-wheelers out this year and low-riders in? Overnight, everyone's cruising Safeway in chopped and channeled low-riders. Are Vuarnet sunglasses out and Oakley Blades in? Hand me my Blades, dude.

At the same time, cherished traditions endure. Slippers are left at the door, mangoes and bananas shared. No one runs if walking will do, and no plate lunch ever includes greens. Whenever possible, one sits in the shade, drives with the left arm extended along the chassis, eats rice for strength and seaweed for longevity.

There are "work jobs" and "fun jobs," and many people have at least one of each. Other cultures, religions and races are respected – but if a joke can be made, it will be.

Food, music, laughter and friendship are more important than power or fame. Money is to be saved, spent on the kids, or gambled with in Vegas. Storytelling is the highest art; pidgin English the language of choice. Cars and trucks are more important than houses. You just live in your house, but you are your ride!

More often than not, your ride will take you to a Maui-style party. No personal milestone: baptism, first birthday, graduation, engagement, marriage, wedding anniversary, promotion or retirement can be allowed to pass without celebration. Small parties (twenty to 100 guests) are held in the carport. Middle-size parties (100 to 1,000) form in parks, union halls, canoe sheds, job sites or community centers. Big parties (1,000 to 4,000) may require hotel ballrooms or major gymnasiums, and family reunions happen whenever they want to. If the party can be staged for charity, as is the Hotel Charity Walk when the whole town strolls the streets, stopping along the way to gossip and eat at street stalls, so much the better.

It is also Maui style for ethnic groups, religions and entire towns to party, often with no more excuse than the anniversary of last year's party. The island's Filipinos host the barrio fiesta, Jose Rizal Day, Miss Sampaguita and Flores de Mayo pageants. The Portuguese pitch annual parish-wide festivals in Makawao (St. Joseph's carnival) and Kula (Holy Ghost Feast). The Japanese host the Chrysanthemum Ball and annual dinners honoring veterans of the famed 442nd infantry battalion of World War II. Maui's Buddhist temples invite all comers to summer O-bon (harvest season) dances honoring the spirits of departed loved ones.

Hawaiian-themed events include parades honoring Prince Jonah Kuhio and King Kamehameha, Lahainaluna School's David Malo Day lū'au and concert, and Hāna's proud Aloha Festival observances. Upcountry residents flock to Seabury Hall school's annual craft fair, Hui No'eau Visual Arts Center's Christmas show, and Oski Rice Arena rodeos during the summer.

Island-wide parties include the Maui County Fair and Maui Jaycee Carnival as well as any rock, reggae or Hawaiian music concert. Popular canoe regattas are staged annually off Kahului, Lahaina and Kīhei; rodeos at Makawao, Hāna and 'Ulupalakua. There are "zoo fests" and "art nights," "whale days" and a wild and crazy Halloween celebration in Lahaina, plus Fourth of July fireworks and Chinese New Year dinners that run for five consecutive nights.

All of this is Maui style, but there's a quieter story as well. A grocer replaces a shopper's dropped bottle of pickles for free, "because she was upset enough already." A young hula dancer performs on one leg, because she has only one. An elderly couple invites a first-time visitor, a stranger, to share picnic dinner at the beach.

That's Maui style.

Pages 42, 43 – Ke'anae
Schoolchildren enjoy recess at Ke'anae School.

Above – Central Maui
A heavy equipment driver stirs up Maui's red dirt
while working in the cane fields.

Right – Kula
During restoration work, the crew takes a break on
the steps of Kula's Chinese Temple.

Facing page – Hāna Highway
"Uncle Harry" Mitchell, November 30, 1919-
November 17, 1991, always had time to "talk story"
on a lazy afternoon.

Facing page – Paukūkalo
The Reverend Torako Arine, a priestess, bows in prayer before the altar of the Jinsha Shinto Shrine.

Left – Kula
The Church of the Holy Ghost provides a reverent retreat for devout catholics of the community.

Above left – Hāna
Hawaiians still hold sacred Pi'ilani Hale Heiau, a temple of stones that holds the *mana*, spiritual reverence, of the past.

Above right – Lahaina
Offerings are neatly placed on the altar of the Chee Kung Tong Society's Wo Hing Temple.

Above – Hāna
The Lono family of Hāna poses for a portrait at a family reunion.

Right – Lahaina
Leis and a straw hat are perfect attire for Maui's tropical climate.

Facing Page – Maui
A Maui smorgesbord of lūʻau food includes kalua pig, tako, lomi lomi salmon, chicken long rice, haupia, Maui onion, red (alae) salt and poi.

Page 52 – Wailea
There's nothing better than a cool ice cream bar on a hot Maui summer day.

Page 53 – Mākena Landing
Someone at every island gathering knows how to strum a guitar.

Facing page – Wailuku
Bubble gum and boys (like Walter Medieros) go
together like baseballs and players' mitts!

Above left – Wailuku
Lively Maui children wave a jubilant greeting as
school lets out for the summer.

Above right – La Perouse
Both fish and Maui *keikis*, children, play peek-a-boo
in tidepools along lava coastline.

Left – Central Maui
Sigudo-san contemplates the world from the
weathered window of his cozy plantation home.

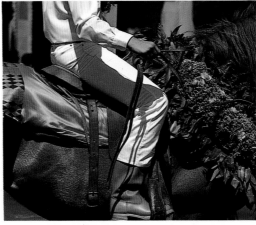

Above – Hāna
Flowers, friends and fun are all part of the Aloha
Festival's parade down main street.

Right – Hāna
A pāʻū rider sits proudly astride his fern-and-flower-
bedecked mount during the parade.

Facing page – Wailea
Even the youngest island dancers have "graceful
hula hands."

Above – Kā'anapali
The hands tell the story of "a million flowers" in this *wahine*, women's, hula.

Right – Kā'anapali
The *kane*, men, dance in yellow malo, kukui nut leis and head leis made of ti leaves.

Facing Page – Wailea
Jill Pascua is all decked out in plumeria flowers to dance at Wailea.

CHAPTER 4

Sea-Born

E nui ke aho, e ku'u keiki, a moe i ke kai, no ke kai la ho'i ka'āina

TAKE A DEEP BREATH MY SON, AND LAY YOURSELF IN THE SEA,

FOR THEN THE LAND SHALL BELONG TO THE SEA

There is a stretch on the 'Ulupalakua road where Maui's relationship to the ocean can be considered. It is a good spot to pause for a while, turn off the radio and absorb the island feeling of this place.

The eye, gliding downward and outward like a bird in flight, soars past cactus-studded pastures and manicured resorts to the open sea beyond. Even from this distance, one thing is clear: the ocean here is not some painted stage prop, flat and still. This ocean is alive.

In the middle distance, crescent-shaped Molokini braves the 'Alalakeiki Channel. A southerly current rips past the islet, leaving standing wakes best seen in the glare of late afternoon. From here, Molokini looks like a dive boat whose anchor barely holds against the sucking current. One slip and the boat will vanish around the corner and bob off toward Tahiti.

Farther offshore, cobalt swells hammer the stark black cliffs of Kaho'olawe, sending salty sheets of spray into the dazzled air. The ocean boils and booms, draws back upon itself, then hammers in again. Borne aloft by the sea wind, ghosts of crushed spray rise to Kaho'olawe's cliff tops and there overlook the famous channel called KealaiKahiki – the road to Tahiti.

From these same cliff tops centuries ago, bonfires licked the night sky, helping mariners set their southward course for 3,000-mile open-ocean voyages to the home islands. Positioned by the bonfires on Lāna'i and Kaho'olawe, it is said, double-hulled voyaging canoes set their sails to the night wind and coursed off into the heaving, trackless dark, returning months later with settlers from Tahiti and the Marquesas.

These ancient journeys, undertaken without celestial instruments of any kind, began at night so that *kahuna*, master navigators, could set their course by the rising and setting stars of the various Pacific Island groups. (One important constellation marking Hawai'i is the Pleiades, known in Polynesia as the "Seven Little Eyes" or "Seven Little Sisters.")

What supreme confidence they possessed, those ocean-going ancestors. They did not separate land from sea in the manner of today. The ocean was as much their home as any rainy windward valley or sun-baked leeward slope.

Today, no voyaging canoes can be seen from the slopes of 'Ulupalakua, but their double-hulled descendents are visible. Trailing creamy wakes, a fleet of churning catamarans ferries visitors to the marine reserve at Molokini.

Modern ocean explorers now ply the waves on foam and fiberglass boards that are aerodynamically designed for speed and balance. Big winter surf draws Maui board surfers to such thrilling breaks as Spreckelsville and Pier One off Kahului, where waves have been ridden at heights of twenty-five feet and higher. Summer surfers head for Ma'alaea, Olowalu and Lahaina, while skim-boarders prefer the shoreline surf at Makena. Kayak surfing and long-distance kayak paddling along Maui's lee shores also have become increasingly popular, but as in early days, the unchallenged favorite ocean activity of long-time residents remains fishing in all its forms.

Scores of other coastal sites on Maui provide safe entry to and exploration of the ocean – notably the coral gardens at Olowalu and Lahaina, Kā'anapali's Black Rock cove near the Sheraton-Maui Hotel, and Hāna's Wai'ānapanapa and Hāmoa beaches. But none matches Molokini's diversity of "sub"-terrain and marine life.

Cradled by the brown arms of a half-sunken caldera, the sand and coral lagoon slopes from four to forty feet in depth. Many of the creatures common to Hawai'i's inland waters can be seen at Molokini, although the islet lies a mile seaward of the nearest shallow coast.

Iridescent wrasses and parrot fish, schools of dainty moorish idols, and crowds of yellow tang and butterflyfish flicker among the coral heads. All the reef fish can be seen here, as can moray eels, octopi, white-tipped sharks, trumpet fish and the colorful, clown-like Hawaiian state fish with the breathtaking name Humuhumunukunukuapua'a.

But what sets Molokini apart from Hawai'i's other undersea destinations is that this offshore volcanic remnant is far enough from land to attract passing pelagic (deep sea) fish as well. Schools of beautiful blue and gold "rainbow runners," seldom seen elsewhere, may surprise divers ascending Molokini's 200-foot deep "back ledge." And snorkelers on the shallower lagoon side may suddenly find themselves encircled by thousands of silvery, tightly-packed baby mackerel.

Eagle rays and even giant manta rays with twelve-foot "wingspans" appear at Molokini and glide past startled viewers like spacecraft from some outer galaxy. Green sea turtles, ruffled jellyfish and feisty snapping shrimp mingle with scuttling slipper lobsters and spiny blowfish in water so clear you can spot a single sea urchin more than 100 feet away.

Water this clear and warm transmits sounds as well as sights, and the incessant snap-crackle-pop of the living reef is a surprise to first-time snorkelers. Those who listen closely underwater may also hear the croaking of goat fish and the "chunk-chunk-chunk" of parrot fish crunching into coral with their bony beaks.

The eeriest and most beautiful sounds in Maui waters also can be heard at Molokini during winter months. These are the booming, keening songs of the humpback whales that migrate from Alaska each year to mate and calve in the waters off Maui. Ranging from deep bass notes to high, pinging squeaks, the songs can be heard from December through April by anyone patient enough to cling to some underwater object and remain silent for a few seconds.

Welsh poet Dylan Thomas recalled a childhood seaside Christmas where "the whole of the sea was hilly with whales," and so it seems off Maui sometimes. All winter long, the ocean explodes like a depth-charge sequence in some old submarine movie as forty-ton humpbacks launch themselves into the air or pound the sea to froth with their massive flukes.

Far subtler, but no less startling, are the sudden flashes of flying fish, silvery wings outspread, as they sail along beside a boat for hundreds of feet before entering the water again. Dolphins, too, accompany vessels off Maui's shores, and it is even possible – though rare – to spot full-grown marlin, spiny sails upraised, leaping through the waves in hot pursuit of prey.

The ancient seafarers who crossed the Pacific between Hawai'i and Tahiti knew all these creatures in all their forms, knew their personalities and preferences, named them, studied them, and put them to every conceivable use. They knew when to catch them, when to let them replenish themselves, and when to offer them up to the gods. They honored them in song, dance and legend.

Gazing down now from the 'Ulupalakua roadside, squinting into the sunlit channel between Molokini and Kaho'olawe, it is possible for a moment to imagine Maui as the old Hawaiians knew it – not land and sea apart, but a truly submersible world where all "the land shall belong to the sea."

Pages 60, 61 – North Kīhei
Canoe paddlers pull together under the setting sun off Sugar Beach.

Facing page – Haleakalā
Visible from the island of Kahoʻolawe, Haleakalā was a point of reference for ancient voyagers.

Above – Mākena
An aerial view of Mākena reveals the serenity of Big and Little Beaches on Maui's southern coast.

Left – Kamaʻole III Beach Park
Two-year-old Erin Wooldrige sets out for a day at the beach.

Above left – Kīhei
A young snorkeler prepares to hit the reef.

Above right – Ho'okipa
A boogie boarder "gets air."

Right – Maui waters
Surfer Buzzy Kerbox travels through "the tube" of a breaking wave.

Facing page – Mākena
A south swell at Mākena supplies perfect waves for skimboarder Doug Edwards.

Above – Kīhei
This colorful fresh catch includes lobster, parrot fish, manini and other reef fish.

Right – Mākena
A lone pole fisherman casts his line from the beach at Mākena.

Facing page – West Maui
Considerable skill is involved in casting a net Hawaiian style so it falls fully extended onto the surface of the ocean.

Above – Molokini
The waters surrounding crescent-shaped Molokini
are alive with colorful reef fish.

Right – Molokini
This subspecies of the fairy basslet fish reaches its
most spectacular appearance in Hawaiian waters.

Far right – Maui waters
Graceful orange tube coral is a familiar sight to
snorkelers and divers swimming near Maui reefs.

Facing page – Molokini
A school of nocturnal raccoon butterflyfish feed near
Molokini.

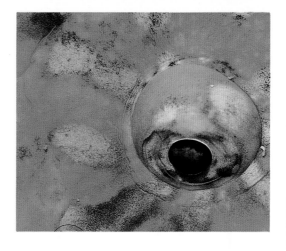

Above left – Molokini
A spiny puffer fish mugs for the camera during a cruise to Molokini.

Above right – Maui waters
Hawai'i's green sea turtles are protected as an endangered species.

Right – Maui waters
This bubble-like nudibranch is only one of many varieties found in Maui waters.

Facing page – West Maui waters
Graceful humpback whales arrive in Maui waters every winter, returning to colder Alaskan climes when March rolls around.

Facing page – Kīhei Beach
Fast-growing Kīhei has become a popular resort and residential area in less than a quarter of a century.

Above – Kīhei
Nothing matches a Kīhei sunset – except perhaps a Wailea, Lahaina, Kā'anapali, Nāpili or Kapalua sunset!

Left – Kīhei
The golden rays of the setting Kīhei sun signal the time for sailboats to head home from the sea.

To the Valleys

'A'ohe o kāhi nānā o luna o ka pali; iho mai a lalo nei; 'ike i ke au nui ke au iki, he alo a he alo

THE TOP OF THE CLIFF ISN'T THE PLACE TO LOOK AT US; COME DOWN HERE AND

LEARN OF THE BIG AND LITTLE CURRENT, FACE-TO-FACE

From ancient times through World War II, virtually all who came to Maui had one thing in common: they arrived by sea. This maritime delivery wasn't everyone's idea of a good time, as generations of seasick settlers have attested, but it did give Mauians a deeper appreciation of their island's scenic and topographic diversity than perceived by many visitors today.

Travelers and new residents arriving by air see Maui as a single island, and a rather uniform one at that. The two mountains are apparent, as is the sugar-planted isthmus linking them, but where are the fabled valleys?

Earlier generations who reached Maui by voyaging canoe, square rigger or steam packet gained a far different first impression. To them, Maui seemed two islands, because the low-lying "saddle" between the mountains practically disappears from a maritime perspective. Of the two volcanic domes that remain, West Maui is clearly the "Valley Isle" of popular song.

From the county seat of Wailuku, a clockwise circuit of West Maui reveals the great eroded clefts that give the Valley Island its nickname: 'Īao Valley, Waikapū, Ukumehame, Olowalu, Kahana, Kahakuloa, Waihe'e and Waiehu. These spectacular gorges and the pristine streams which carved them radiate like spokes from the jungled hub of West Maui's crater, Pu'ukukui. The annual rainfall at this ancient caldera's center ranks with the world's highest; its walls are among the steepest and loftiest in the Pacific.

So bountiful is West Maui's rainfall – up to 420 inches annually – that the state and federal governments have spent tens of millions of dollars in recent years building massive flood control channels near Wailuku and Lahaina.

Though costly, the work is warranted. In the early years of this century, an 'Īao Stream flash flood destroyed the village of Spanish Camp and swept inhabitants to their deaths. Lahaina also has been severely flooded several times by rainfall runoff from Kahoma Stream, now girded in $32 million worth of concrete.

This same rainfall, capable of immense damage in a short time, can also carve geologic masterpieces, given enough time. At two million years of age, West Maui produced such wonders as ʻIao Valley and Ukumehame Canyon as well as the narrower crevasses of Olowalu, Waikapū and Waiheʻe. ʻIao Valley, in the shadow of 1,200-foot ʻIao Needle, figures prominently in Maui's history, for it was here that King Kamehameha I battled the army of Maui's Chief Kalanikupule. For the first time in Hawaiʻi, a Western weapon – a cannon – was fired. So many bodies filled the valley stream that it came to be known as *Kepaniwai* , the damming of the waters. Today, the guava-strewn, ginger-scented footpaths leading to ʻIao Stream and its several sparkling swimming holes are popular with hikers and island youths, who can be found on any warm afternoon making cannon-ball entries from the surrounding cliffs into pools below.

The streams that formed these scenic declivities no longer run to the sea as they once did, having for the past century been diverted for irrigation. The waters of Waiheʻe, ʻIao and Waikapū streams now feed the pineapple and macadamia nut crops of Wailuku Agribusiness. The streams that carved Ukumehame and Olowalu valleys water Pioneer Mill sugar crops, and the waters of Kahana and Kahakuloa irrigate pineapple fields for Maui Land & Pineapple Company. Like their counterparts on Haleakalā, the streams of West Maui were harnessed for commercial use by an ingenious system of dams, tunnels and flumes built during the last quarter of the nineteenth century and the first few years of the twentieth. Capturing the stream flow near its mountain sources, these irrigation networks enabled early planters to make previously barren coastal regions bloom.

The idea that the same land mass could be described in one breath as both "barren" and "among the wettest places on Earth" is a trick of island geography. Like all "high islands" swept by moisture-laden trade winds, Maui has a greener, wetter side (the northeast, or windward shore) and a browner, drier side (the southwest, or leeward shore). In addition, West Maui also displays marked climatic variations from summit to shore, with its peaks catching far more rainfall than its coasts.

This is because West Maui, in effect, generates its own weather. Evaporatory moisture rising from the ocean and from Maui's wetter slopes forms clouds each day at an altitude of about 6,000 feet. Because West Maui is precisely that high, water from the clouds wreathing its peaks condenses back down into the "bowl" of Puʻukukui's crater. From there it tumbles downward and seaward through West Maui's valleys, diminishing as it approaches the coast.

That is partly why West Maui has valleys along its entire circumference, while Haleakalā's valleys fall largely on its windward (weather-facing) side. At 10,000 feet, the larger mountain's summit rises far above the 6,000-foot cloud layer, so Haleakalā does not enjoy the "radial erosion" process that has made its older brother so visually and topographically distinctive. Instead, the East Maui summit usually stays dry, and the clouds that gather at Haleakalā's 6,000-foot mark do different things on opposite sides of the mountain. On the windward side, they release rain into the high forests and watersheds of Waikamoi and Hāna district. On the leeward side, from Kaikinui to about Pukalani, mist and occasional dense fog forms – but nothing like the 420 inches of rain recorded on West Maui.

West Maui's meteorology also favored its various planters and commercial developers, who did not have to bring water very far from any particular source. Thus, sugar grown at Olowalu could be watered from Olowalu. On all arcs of West Maui's "circle" were streams and valleys, and irrigation water rarely had to be diverted more than a few miles from its source. This was not the case on East Maui, where water captured in the forests above Kailua, Keʻanae and Nāhiku must travel more than thirty miles to reach its destination: the 50,000 acres of cane planted in Maui's saddle and along Haleakalā's western slopes.

The ready availability of stream water and the greater range of climatic conditions occurring over a short distance also gave West Maui a leg up on Haleakalā with respect to settlement patterns. With the possible exception of Hāna, which enjoys optimal rainfall year-round, populations were far likelier to form near the temperate valleys and fertile alluvial fans of West Maui than along Haleakalā's flanks, one of which gets too much rain, the other too little to suit most settlers.

West Maui thus has drawn to itself much of the political, economic and commercial clout generated on Maui through the centuries, and its relative proximity to Lānaʻi, Molokaʻi and Oʻahu also has enhanced its strategic importance. Wailuku and Lahaina were historically prominent centuries before East Maui communities such as Kīhei, Pāʻia and Wailea rose from the red dirt.

Pages 76, 77 – ʻĪao Valley
Tranquil ʻĪao Valley is the site where the invading
King Kamehameha the Great once defeated the
Maui forces.

Facing page – Puʻunēnē
In the foreground, a Maui man clears a stream the
old way, while in the background smoke pours from
the stacks of a computerized sugar factory.

Above – Waikapū Valley
Loaded with sugar cane, trucks barrel through the
fields along unpaved "cane haul" roads.

Left – Honokōwai
Dried leaves and waste products are burned from the
fields of cane, leaving only the sugar-rich stalks to
harvest.

Facing page – Waiehu
Much of the harvesting of pineapple is still accomplished by workers who hand pick the fruit in the fields.

Left – Central Maui
The first pineapples were introduced to the islands about thirty-five years after Captain Cook's arrival and by the 1850s were frequently traded to visiting whalers.

Above – Hāna Highway
A roadside fruit stand displays pineapples, bananas, melons, grapes, nectarines and mangos.

Above left – Wailuku
Crowds turn out to watch the battle of the monster
trucks, first held at War Memorial Park.

Above right – Wailuku
Kaʻahumanu Church, built in 1876, conducts Sunday
services in Hawaiian.

Facing page – Central Maui
Red dirt, green cane and exuberant youth are all part
of the Maui way of life.

Facing page – ʻĪao Needle
ʻĪao Needle reaches 1,200 feet into the sky, standing
as a tranquil sentinel to historic ʻĪao Valley.

Above left – ʻĪao Valley
Kepaniwai (the damming of the waters) Stream is
said to have been clogged with bodies after a battle
fought by the invading King Kamehameha the Great.

Above right – ʻĪao Valley
Chameleons as green as the ʻĪao foliage can change
their color to match their habitat.

Left – ʻĪao Valley
Sunlight and shadows highlight the linear lines of a
fan palm.

Facing page – Waiehu Valley
A swinging bridge is the quickest route through
Waiehu Valley.

Above left – West Maui Mountains
After a heavy shower, countless waterfalls fall from
West Maui ridges.

Above right – Hāna
Early Hawaiians used amau fern fronds as mulch for
taro, as pillow stuffing, and in times of famine, as food.

Left – Twin Falls
Fallen mountain apple blossoms blanket the forest
floor, turning the ground red.

A Royal Playground

CHAPTER 6

E lauhoe mai na wa'a; i ke kā, i ka hoe; i ka hoe, i ke kā; pae aku i ka'aina

EVERYBODY PADDLE THE CANOES TOGETHER; BAIL AND PADDLE,

PADDLE AND BAIL, AND THE SHORE IS REACHED

f all Maui's historic communities, none was so prominent as Lahaina, whose pleasing weather and broad, sheltering lee made it a favorite of Hawaiian chiefs and royalty as far back as the fifteenth century. The great sixteenth-century monarch Pi'ilani so esteemed Lahaina and its northern environs that several West Maui bays were designated "the bays of Pi'ilani" (Honoapi'ilani), a name now borne by the highway that rings West Maui.

Hawai'i's greatest ruler, Kamehameha I, built the first western-style structure the kingdom had ever seen in 1802 at Lahaina. This "brick palace" housed Kamehameha and two of his sons, their wives and retinues during the royal court's sojourn to Maui. Lahaina thus enjoyed the distinction of serving as unofficial capital of the Hawaiian kingdom until Kamehameha III moved the monarchy to Honolulu in the 1840s.

Though the brick palace no longer exists, many other handsomely restored structures attest to Lahaina's importance as a political and commercial center as well as its social stature as a playground for royalty. Historic buildings open to today's visitors include the Seamen's Hospital (1830s); Maui's first stone church, Waiola Protestant (1832); Lahainaluna School printing house (1834); and the missionary home of the Reverend Dwight and Charlotte Baldwin (1838). The Maria Lanakila Catholic Church dates from 1858, though the present building is a 1928 replacement. Other venerable landmarks include the downtown banyan tree (planted in 1873 and still growing strong), Pioneer Inn (1901) and the Wo Hing Society temple (1912). Less venerable, but no less important, are the town's Hongwanji and Jodo Missions, the latter fronting a 7,000-pound Buddha figure deemed the largest outside Hawai'i.

The history surrounding these buildings includes some of Maui's seminal events. The island's first Congregational missionaries arrived in Lahaina in 1823, shortly after Kamehameha's death, and soon converted the powerful regent Queen Ka'ahumanu to Christianity. Ka'ahumanu in turn spearheaded the toppling of Hawai'i's ancient *kapu*, taboo, system that had defined the social order for a thousand years. She persuaded the king, Liholiho, to host a public feast where men and women sat together and women ate foods previously allowed only to men, thus breaking the kapu.

New England whaling ships started arriving in 1820 and wintered off Lahaina in varying numbers for the next fifty years. At the whaling industry's peak in the 1840s and 1860s, as many as 400 ships annually swung at anchor in Lahaina's flat and windless "road stead." Construction of Hale Pa'ahao Prison was actually deemed necessary to contain raucous sailors in 1852.

The first high school west of the Rocky Mountains was founded at Lahainaluna in 1831. The printing press there disseminated the first written form of the Hawaiian language, enabling scholars like David Malo to record the swiftly vanishing beliefs and customs of an older Hawai'i. Lahainaluna School also produced many of the kingdom's first western-educated jurists and religious and government leaders.

These worthies did battle with Lahaina's rowdy whaling crews for decades, until the discovery of petroleum in Pennsylvania in the 1870s doomed the North Pacific fisheries that had thrived chiefly from the distillation of whale oils for illumination. Its greatest historical epoch behind it, Lahaina settled into the more mundane calling of plantation town for Pioneer Mill Company. Except for some precedent-setting labor union activity during the 1930s and 1940s – including a pivotal role in the revolutionary territory-wide sugar strike of 1946 – Lahaina reclined in easy slumber for nearly a century after the whalers left.

As recently as statehood (1959), the island's plantation-based economy was moribund at best. The pineapple industry was losing money, sugar was barely holding its own, and Maui's young people were leaving in droves to seek work in Honolulu or on the U.S. mainland.

Yet just ninety-eight miles north, O'ahu was experiencing a boom in tourism, construction and real estate activity unequalled in Pacific history. Not surprisingly, Maui's leaders wondered if they might be able to beckon even a fraction of that business their way.

Then in 1963, the opening of Hawai'i's first "destination resort" at Kā'anapali jolted Lahaina out of its doldrums and set West Maui onto an extraordinary new course as a purveyor of sunshine and relaxation to the world. In addition to standard resort offerings like tennis, golf, pool swimming, shuffleboard and hula lessons, many hotel activity desks now post a full list of off-property recreation choices for Maui visitors.

The corporate owners of Kā'anapali had the foresight to separate the resort from the nearby town of Lahaina. In light of its heritage as a former capital of the Hawaiian kingdom and an important terminus for early whalers, merchants and missionaries, Lahaina was designated an historic district. From an economic standpoint, the dual attractions proved irresistible. Spurred by the success of its flagship hotel, the Sheraton-Maui, Kā'anapali soon attracted discerning visitors and savvy investors. A dozen other hotel and condominium projects followed, and Kā'anapali became a billion-dollar property. It also acted as a venture capital magnet for the rest of Maui, setting the stage for three other major resorts, more than 200 condominium projects and hundreds of luxury estates that would rise during the 1970s and 1980s.

Lahaina, meanwhile, was getting a major make-over of its own. Aware that Kā'anapali's visitors would need someplace to shop and sightsee, the town fathers converted their sleepy, red dirt, plantation-era outpost into a smart and spanky setup of a New England whaling seaport, complete with its own square-rigged brig. Before long, two million tourists a year were ambling happily up and down Front Street.

The town became identified with whales. Not only did the great marine mammals cavort just offshore each winter, their images filled half the shops in Lahaina. Ivory carvers flocked to Front Street by the score, making that colorful avenue America's scrimshaw capital and an important reliquary for one of the nation's bona fide folk arts. Whale books and posters filled shop windows, and every block had a harpooner's saloon or old whaler's grog shoppe. Kā'anapali chose a spouting whale as its logo and established an outdoor whaling museum as the centerpiece for its shopping mall.

Lahaina's significant role in Hawaiian history spurred some interest in island-themed fine art, fabrics and handicrafts, but it was the whaling association that truly caught the attention of Maui shoppers. Soon marine art – paintings, sculptures and historic lithographs – became the cornerstone of a new retail art empire. From November through May, "whale watch" cruises depart from Lahaina, Kā'anapali, Mā'alaea and Wailea. Deep-sea fishing trips and sailing expeditions depart each morning from Mā'alaea and Lahaina harbors, and "sunset dinner cruises" ply the same sea lanes each night. Glass bottom boats tour Lahaina's reefs, and half-day snorkel and dive trips head for Lānaʻi, Molokini and points unknown.

Visitors and residents alike love the beaches and water activities of the southwest coast. Windsurf lessons can be had at Kanahā, Māʻalaea and Kaʻanapali; kayak surfing at Olowalu. The island's most famous winter surfing break is Honolua Bay on West Maui. Huge, clean, picture-perfect waves peel off along this bay's northern flank drawing surfers from all around the world.

Yet, this modern Polynesian playground still retains a traditional *ōhana*, family, awareness. Two of the best attended Lahaina events are the Kamehameha Day parade, when flower-bedecked floats and *pāʻu* riders, women in colorful long skirts on horseback, and high school marching bands turn out on Front Street; and the children's Halloween Parade, which draws hundreds of costumed kids annually.

In the spring, families flock to Na Mele O Maui, Kāʻanapali's annual festival celebrating Hawaiian culture, which features a song competition by Maui's school children as well as a hula festival and arts and crafts fair. At mid-summer, families again turn out for the Fourth of July parade and concert, a no-alcohol, outdoor event highlighting the Maui Symphony.

Resort development continues to spread across the west end of Maui expanding popular destinations such as Nāpili and Kapalua with upscale hotels. Boarded by the blue ocean on one side and acres of manicured golf courses on the other, Kapalua is the emerald in the crown of West Maui's resorts. Appropriate activities are scheduled annually to keep present-day revelers returning to this favored playground year after year. Besides the Kapalua Open Tennis and the Kapalua Invitational Golf tournaments, music lovers can indulge themselves for two long weekends at the Kapalua Music Festival every June, and oenophiles can do the same during the Kapalua Wine Symposium each July.

While Mauians and visitors generally enjoy separate recreational tracks, the island's jumping nightlife draws everyone together after hours. Discos at the major resorts teem nightly with islanders and conventioneers, while in Lahaina, turn-away crowds throng Front Street's dance clubs and Hard Rock Café. There is more than enough happening on this island to burst the "Polynesian paralysis" picture for all time. These days the thing most visitors need after a vacation on Maui is – a vacation.

Pages 90, 91 – Lahaina Harbor
The brig *Cartheginian II* is a replica of the type
of ship that brought the missionaries around Cape
Horn to Hawai'i in the early 1800s.

Left – Lahaina Harbor
The West Maui Mountains form a familiar backdrop
for the tall masts of the sailing ships docked in
Lahaina Harbor.

Above – Lahaina
Bathed in the golden rays of the afternoon sun, many
of Front Street's historic buildings date from the
1800s, others have been built to look as if they
predate 1920.

Above left – Lahaina
Pioneer Inn, built in 1920, is a popular Lahaina
gathering place with a restaurant and bar that capture
the ambience of the whaling era.

Above right – Lahaina
This "old salt" keeps watch over shoppers strolling
past Lahaina storefronts.

Right – Lahaina
Scrimshaw, artful carving and engraving on whale
ivory, was a leisure-time activity practiced by early
sea-faring whalers.

Left – Lahaina
The Buddha at Jodo Mission Cultural Park commemorates the arrival of the first Japanese to Maui in 1868 and is the largest Buddha to be found outside Japan.

Above – Lahaina
The shrine at Jodo Mission Cultural Park on Pu'unoa Point near Malo Wharf is one of Lahaina's busiest visitor attractions.

Above left – Lahaina
Ghosts, goblins and revelers throng Lahaina's Front Street during Halloween.

Above right – Lahaina
Youngsters get into the spirit of a Fourth of July pie-eating contest.

Right – Lahaina
May Day is Lei Day with lots of flowers, music, ethnic dances and good things to eat at Kamehameha School.

Facing page – Kā'anapali
Competitors in the wild and zany Carole Kai Bedrace dash to do their best for charitable causes.

Above – Kā'anapali
The golf course at Kā'anapali is doubly blessed with twin rainbows stretching across the greens.

Right – Wailua
Hawai'i's own, David Ishii shows the form that won him the Hawaiian Open in 1990.

Far right – Kā'anapali
The crowd cheers as this professional golfer gets out of the sand.

Facing page – Honolua Bay
Sailboaters moor in Honolua to snorkel and enjoy the unspoiled tranquility of the bay.

Above – Kāʻanapali
The long shadows of late afternoon signal the end of another perfect day of sailing.

Right – Lahaina
Sun sets on the sailboats anchored in Lahaina Harbor.

Facing page – Lahaina
Sunset is an ideal time indulge in a dinner cruise on the placid waters off Lahaina.

CHAPTER 7

Through the Artist's Eye

Kamaʻilio ka waha, hana ka lima

LET THE MOUTH TALK, WHILE THE HANDS WORK

*N*owhere does Maui show her colors more brilliantly than in the arts. Here Mauians have flourished, from ethnic and cottage arts and crafts to the ultra-sophisticated galleries (and price tags) of Lahaina, where an ever-growing demand continues to rival markets from New York to Los Angeles. So much, in fact, that Maui has become known as an international art mecca.

Islanders have always had a rich crafts heritage and an appreciation for beauty. The ancient Hawaiians believed that the creative expression of any art form was guided by *aka*, the spirit, and the artisans were considered holy people. The process of creating art, therefore, imbued both the art and its creator with *mana*, spiritual powers.

Ethnologists believe the first Polynesians to arrive in Hawaiʻi brought with them one flowering plant, the *ʻawapuhi*, wild ginger, from which to create decorative leis and headdresses. Seeds, bones, dog, shark and whale teeth, feathers and braided human hair were also used to fashion adornments for the body. Traditional Polynesian arts of canoe building, using stone adzes to hollow out solid koa logs; *kiʻi*, tiki, carvings from wood and stone; body tattooing; fine feather work; hula dancing and chanting; *lau hala*, pandanus, weaving; *kapa* pounding and weapons making were all practiced on Maui, as was the etching of petroglyphs into lava fields and cliff faces.

Even cloth making, was elevated to a symbolic art form. *Kapa*, pounded bark cloth, which celebrated life as a receiving blanket at birth, became a burial shroud upon death. It was each man's identity and testimony of being. In royal families, a child's umbilical cord was wrapped in kapa that had been fashioned especially for him and safely stored until, upon death, his bones were similarly wrapped. Kapa was decorated with intricate patterns colored red, brown and black with natural plant dyes. Like most Hawaiian crafts, it was an art of precision, tradition and time-consuming process. In ancient Hawaiian legend there is a phrase *"Nui la luhi o na wāhine kuku kapa,"* which means, "Great is the weariness of the women who beat kapa."

Other arts included baskets woven of the aerial roots of ʻieʻie, which sported decorative touches made by dyeing the unwoven strips black and brown, requiring the artist to plan the weaving technique in advance. Similar dyeing techniques were used to beautify sleeping mats woven of *makaloa*, sedge, from the island of Niʻihau. Early Hawaiian bowls and gourd water containers were enlivened with handsome geometric patterns painted by hand, and long-ago carvers artistically patched cracks by tapping figure-eight-shaped pieces of wood into matching depressions cut across the split.

Hawaiians were also acclaimed for their fine feather work, creating royal capes from thousands of colorful birds that were captured and later released. A single cloak would take years, sometimes generations, for many hands to complete. Most impressive of all the ancient arts, however, and perhaps the rarest are the carvings of Hawaiian gods found in the *heiau*, temples.

Sadly, most Hawaiian arts were lost in the 1800s with the coming of Westerners. Religious carvings, dances and chants were interpreted by Westerners as idolatry and paganism. Hula was forbidden and the *mele*, chants, were silenced. *Kahuna*, priests, and *kahuna kālai*, carvers were forbidden their art. Dissenters were forced into hiding and their works destroyed. Today only 146 authentic Hawaiian *ki'i*, tikis, remain to guide the work of modern artisans.

With today's artistic greening of Maui has come a renaissance of Hawaiian art throughout the state, supported by such outspoken proponents as Rocky Kai'iouliokahihikoloehu Jensen. Jensen is best known for his dramatic wood sculptures reminiscent of ancient figures, fashioned not only from sennit, koa and kapa, but from such modern materials as nylon cord, wicker, brass, stainless steel and ceramics.

In 1976, Jensen founded Hale Naua III, the Society of Hawaiian Artists, providing native islanders an outlet through which they could pool their knowledge of the remnants of their culture. Among the 150-members of Hale Naua (loosely translated as "House of Pedigree,") are a number of Maui artists, including Al Lagunero, Terry Murata and Will Herrera.

With new philosophies introduced since the 1800s, came new skills. In 1920, missionaries introduced converts to quilt making, oil painting and printing techniques on the kingdom's first printing press. Each consecutive wave of immigrants added new capabilities to the island's artistic treasury: stringed musical instruments from Portugal and Spain, calligraphy from China, the whimsical paper-folding art of origami from Japan, and folk dances and dramas from Korea and Okinawa. Eventually, artists sailed into Lahaina Harbor and stayed, entranced by a warm welcome as well as the enthralling play of light and color on the tropical landscape and a booming artistic economy.

In 1934, Ethel Baldwin formed Hui No'eau Visual Arts Center. Now housed in Ethel and Henry Baldwin's beautiful upcountry estate, Kalua Nui, the Hui continues to offer classes in a broad spectrum of artistic interests to the people of Maui. Workshops are on site, and continuing exhibits by local artists are presented daily except Sunday.

In the 1950s, with tourism in its infancy, Lahaina artists took it upon themselves to display their wares along the sea wall or in the park next to historic Pioneer Inn. Fifteen years later, Lahaina Arts Society was formed, and it has been promoting and sustaining local artists ever since. For the last twenty years, through the efforts of such enthusiasts as George Allan, the Lahaina Arts Society has called the old Jail House (under the famous Banyan Tree) home. Many of Maui's most successful artists literally began their island careers in the old jailhouse.

With the boom in tourism came the boom in arts. The former little whaling village turned its fame toward capturing these gentle giants on canvas, in bronze and limited editions rather than by harpoon. Maui became the birthplace of the underwater/overwater, two-world concept made famous by marine artist Robert Lyn Nelson. Maui is also home to Wyland, international whaling wall enthusiast, and renowned marine artist Christian Riese Lassen. Wailea hosts the annual Marine Art Expo, and each winter, Lahaina Galleries hosts the Ocean Art Festival; both contribute to global marine conservation efforts.

Today, a walk along Front Street quickly introduces strollers to a diverse and sophisticated art market. The works of local artists, many who command broad acclaim, may be viewed beside works of Erté, Dali, Picasso and Chagall. The art of modern-day greats such as Peter Max, Andy Warhol and Keith Haring, hangs proudly next to that of Haikū painter and sculptor Piero Resta. In 1989, Lahaina established "Friday Night Is Art Night," with participating galleries presenting special showings, strolling minstrels and complimentary refreshments to attract Front Street patrons. Each year, the Art Maui juried exhibition (held in March) grows finer, and today many Maui hotels house art collections that rival museum collections.

The Maui Community Arts and Cultural Center, a $22-million, fifteen-acre art and cultural complex in Kahului, shepherded by Pundy Yokouchi, is soon to be completed with proceeds from grass-roots donations and corporate gifts. The Center has been a joint vision brought to reality by a dedicated art community, proving again that Maui's true colors do indeed shine most brilliantly in the arts.

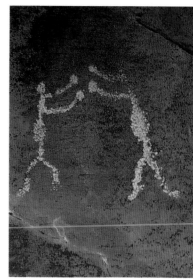

Pages 104, 105 – Upcountry
Jan Kasprzycki works on *Water Lilies*, two mixed-media panals.

Facing page – Lahaina
The weaving of *lau hala* baskets continues to be practiced by artisans to this day.

Above left – Upcountry
Fiber artist Pua Van Dorpe creates kapa and decorative art pieces from natural materials.

Above right – Kalialinui Gulch
Early Hawaiians etched petroglyphs on lava flows.

Far left and left– Hemmeter Collection
Early Hawaiians decorated tools and untensils with patterns etched or painted with natural dyes.
Lei niho pala'oa, a royal pendant of whale ivory and braided human hair is from the eighteenth century.

Above left – Upcountry
Ceramist Tom Faught finishes shaping one of his
oversized vases in his home studio.

Above right – Upcountry
Some Kine Fish, a watercolor by Upcountry artist
Eddie Flotte.

Right – Lahaina
Pua Kea, an oil-on-canvas painting by Lahaina artist
George Allan.

Facing page – Maui
Woman with Hard Hat II, an oil-on-canvas painting
by artist Macario Pascual.

Above – Maui
Chasing Rainbows, a hand-pulled lithograph by
Guy Buffet.

Right – Makawao
Besides offering a wide variety of art classes, Hui
Noeau sponsors Art Maui, a prestigious juried show
of work by island artists.

Above – Maui
Take Home Maui, an oil-on-canvas painting by
Lowell Mapes.

Left – Lahaina
"Friday Night is Art Night" when all the galleries
open their doors, serve *pupus*, hors d'oeuvres, and
wine and art lovers throng Front Street.

Above left – Upcountry
Sardinian Summer, an acrylic-on-canvas painting by
Piero Resta.

Above right – Molokini
Molokini First Breath, a mixed-media limited edition
by marine artist Robert Lyn Nelson.

Right – Kapalua
Kapalua Bay, an oil-on-canvas painting by
Marian Freeman.

Facing page – Kapalua
Kapalua, an oil-on-canvas painting by
Pamela Andelin.

ANDELIN

A Delicate Balance

CHAPTER 8

Ua mau ke ea o ka ʻāina i ka pono

THE LIFE OF THE LAND IS PERPETUATED IN RIGHTEOUSNESS

With its mild temperatures, abundant rainfall and many microclimates, Maui has welcomed thousands of botanical "settlers" since it first broke into the sunlight eons ago. Hawaiʻi's first green, growing things may have arrived the way its first humans did, borne ashore by currents and trade winds after an ocean voyage of at least 3,000 miles. The coconut that colonized a million square miles of the Pacific is just one of many oceanic plants whose tough, buoyant seeds can weather months or even years at sea.

Maui and the other islands in the chain also could have been forested by migratory birds depositing fertile seeds from faraway sources onto Hawaiʻi's porous lava and crushed coral. Other plant species may have arrived as tiny spores drifting down from the jet stream.

Whatever their conveyance, Hawaiʻi's early plants and the creatures that lived among them became some of the world's unique. As the most isolated island group on Earth, Hawaiʻi was denied for most of its natural history the cross-fertilization that led to homogeneity elsewhere.

Instead, Hawaiʻi's plants developed separately from their parent strains, evolving into distinct new species suited to island soils, terrain and weather patterns. The showy silverswords that grow only on Haleakalā and the Big Island are among the best-known botanical examples of this; the nēnē goose a popular avian exponent.

While marine organisms that developed in Hawaiian waters remain relatively unscathed, many of the archipelago's indigenous plants, insects, birds and mammals have not survived human colonization. Enough others are perilously close to extinction to earn Hawaiʻi the sad title of "endangered-species capital of the world." Seventy-two percent of all plant and animal extinctions recorded in the U.S. have occurred in Hawaiʻi. In addition, in 1991, fifteen plant species were added to the endangered and threatened species list by the federal government. It is believed that all have their largest or best-known population on Maui.

Because the Hawaiians had no written language before the nineteenth century, it is difficult to know what flora and fauna were already established in the islands when the first voyaging canoes showed up from Tahiti and the Marquesas. If biologists had time machines, pre-contact Hawaiʻi would be high on their list of research destinations, for even Darwin's fabled Galapagos Islands could not have showcased natural selection so dramatically.

Once the Polynesians discovered Hawai'i, the native flora and fauna started fighting a swift and ultimately futile rear-guard action against invaders from other worlds. Despite a proud tradition of resources conservation that included capturing live birds such as the 'i'iwi and the 'ō'ō to gather feathers to make elaborate feather capes and other chiefly finery and then releasing the birds, the Hawaiians probably destroyed some species outright, altering lowland habitats for planting taro and possibly devouring several populations of flightless birds.

Hardy introduced plants like the banana, sugar cane, taro and yam varieties that arrived in Polynesian voyaging canoes displaced some native flora, and indigenous insects were likewise out-competed by new arrivals. Dogs and pigs that arrived with the Polynesians cut a lethal swath through island bird and plant life that continues today.

The process accelerated in the eighteenth century as traders and settlers from Europe, Asia and the Americas followed in British explorer Captain James Cook's wake to the then-Sandwich Islands. As each ship dropped anchor, species of plants, insects, birds and animals previously unknown to Hawai'i raced ashore.

The ecological damage is ongoing to this day. Goats, cattle and sheep introduced by Captain George Vancouver, as gifts to various chiefs, so overgrazed the islands that precious top soil started blowing and washing away. Even today, after decades of forestry and watershed management, miles of heavily silted shoreline are evident along the lees of all islands.

Far more damaging in the long run was the loss of habitat that accompanied the islands' military, commercial and residential development. Lowland forests that once carpeted the islands vanished long ago – burned and logged for sandalwood and borne away in the holds of China-bound traders. As forests were burned for pastures, wetlands filled in for shopping centers and sand dunes bulldozed for golf courses, Hawai'i's indigenous flora and fauna has been driven closer to extinction. Fewer than twenty Hawaiian crows survive on the Big Island, a situation the State Division of Forestry and Wildlife is trying to remedy through a breeding program at the Endangered Species Propagation Facility at Olinda, Maui. Many native plants are now found alive only in botanical gardens.

The "up" side is that centuries of immigration have endowed Hawai'i with some of the world's most prized flowering shrubs, hardwoods, ornamental plants, pasture grasses and fruit trees. Mountains denuded by the rapacious sandalwood trade of the nineteenth century and by grazing cattle now abound with magnificent rain forest trees from all the tropic and semi-tropic regions of the Pacific Rim.

Introduced plants have long been an economic staple in the islands, from taro that came with the Polynesians, sugar cane and pineapple brought by the Spanish to such recent acquisitions as Napa Valley wine grapes, carnations, sweet onions and the showy South African blooms called protea. All are now cornerstones for Maui export industries.

While environmental awareness has come too late for many of Hawai'i's indigenous species, a growing conservation movement sparked by groups like the Sierra Club, the Audubon Society and The Nature Conservancy is curbing the state's more egregious ecological abuses. On Maui alone, The Nature Conservancy, working in partnership with business, government, organizations and individuals, has set aside three preserves. Waikamoi is a high elevation rain forest that shelters twelve Hawaiian bird species, seven of them endangered. At Kapunakea Preserve in the West Maui mountains, at least twenty-five different types of rare Hawaiian plants, animals and natural communities such as land snails are protected on 13,000 contiguous acres. And the Maui Lava Tubes house a unique species of cave insects found only in this fragile Maui ecosystem. International wildlife groups also have rallied to the defense of Hawai'i's imperiled sea turtles, monk seals, humpback whales, crows, geese and rain forests. But even as these rescue efforts proceed, all islands face tremendous development pressures driven by steadily deteriorating environmental conditions elsewhere.

Maui faces a world-class environmental challenge, but the island also offers long-term research sites in an incredible range of accessible habitats. With the world's increasing awareness of the need to work together to save our planet's resources, hope grows that the complex biological problems of tropical ecosystems can be explored and new techniques developed to manage them. By solving its own problems, Maui can serve as an example for embattled environments everywhere – a fitting role for a special island where people draw memory, custom, knowledge and vision from the land.

Pages 116, 117 – Pāʻia
Vanda orchids are an income-producing crop, used
profusely in orchid leis.

Facing page – Maui
Floating leaves and large, showy purple blossoms
characterize the water lilies found in Hawaiʻi.

Far left and left – Maui
Croton, in addition to being an ornamental plant, has
medicinal qualities.
Torch ginger grows wild throughout the islands.

Above left – Maui
The fragrant yellow flowers of the plumeria are often
strung into homemade leis.

Above right – Maui
No tropical bouquet would be complete without a
heliconia or two gracing the arrangement.

Above – Maui
The yellow hibiscus is Hawai'i's official state flower.

Right – Maui
Bird of paradise, originally from southern Africa, has
showy orange blossoms that resemble a bird in flight.

Facing page – West Maui
Valleys in the West Maui mountains are filled with
ferns and foliage, wild orchids and blossoming lehua.

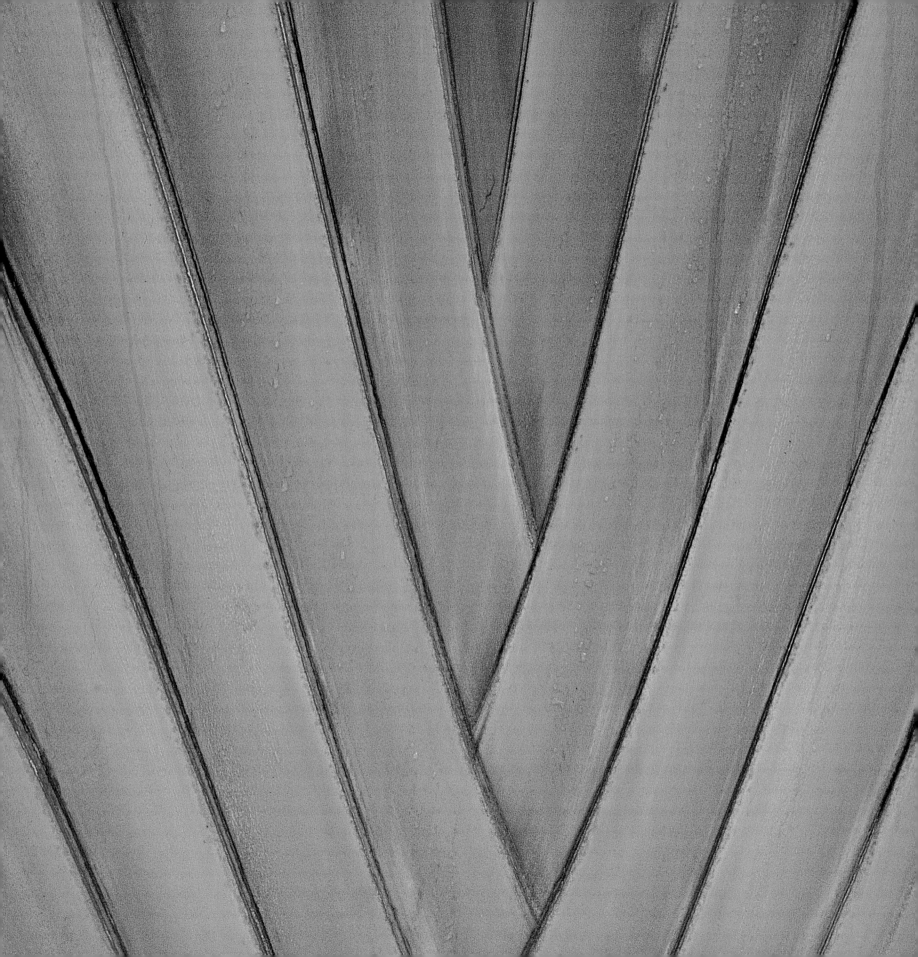

Facing page – Maui
The miraculous order of nature is evident in the striated pattern of a fan palm.

Above left – Waikamoi Preserve
Dew sparkles on branches draped with moss and spider webs in the misty depths of the rain forest.

Above right – Kīpahulu
Waterfalls thunder from the cliffs after a heavy downpour at Kīpahulu.

Left – Maui
A single jade-green fern frond contrasts with brushy undergrowth.

Above left – Kīpahulu Valley
Once abundant, Hawaiian tree snails are becoming
increasingly rare.

Above right – Hosmer Grove
Early Hawaiians used the bright red feathers of the
ʻiʻiwi bird, or scarlet Hawaiian honeycreeper (shown
here on an ʻohia tree), in feather work.

Right – East Maui
The *ʻapapane*, another Hawaiian honeycreeper, has a
crimson body with black wings and tail.

Facing page – Ukumehame Valley
Tree ferns grow in lush profusion in many of Maui's
cooler valleys and rain forests.

Above – Upcountry
A *pueo*, the short-eared Hawaiian owl, was considered a benevolent *aumakua*, personal god, in early Hawai'i.

Right – Haleakalā
Two rare silverswords in full bloom are part of a grouping of five growing in close proximity.

Far right – Haleakalā
In the sun, the leaves of the silversword glisten as if they were artificially brushed with metallic silver paint.

Facing page – West Maui
Afternoon mist veils the lush foliage of Hanaula Tropical Rain Forest.

Maui

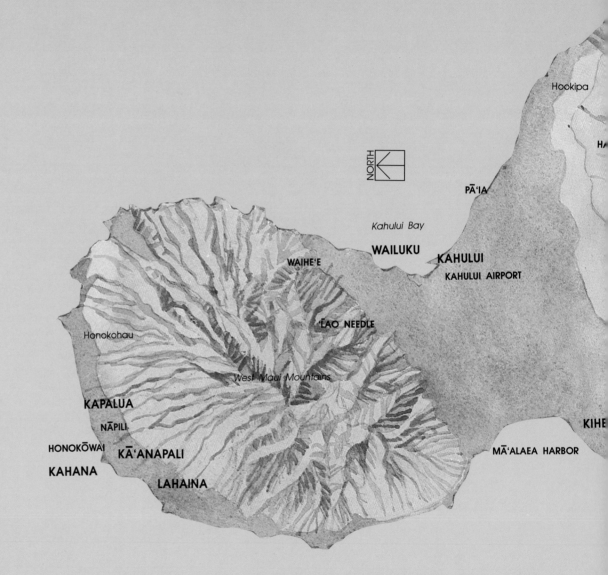

NORTH

Hookipa

PĀ'IA

HA

Kahului Bay

WAILUKU

KAHULUI

WAIHE'E

KAHULUI AIRPORT

'IAO NEEDLE

Honokohau

West Maui Mountains

KAPALUA

NĀPILI

KIHE

HONOKŌWAI

KĀ'ANAPALI

MĀ'ALAEA HARBOR

KAHANA

LAHAINA

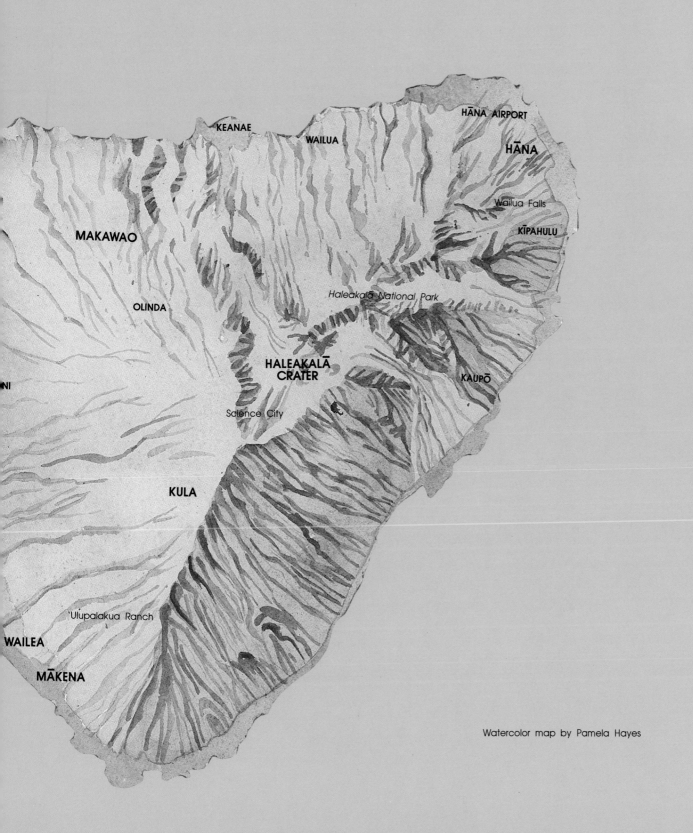

KEANAE

WAILUA

HĀNA AIRPORT

HĀNA

MAKAWAO

Wailua Falls

KĪPAHULU

OLINDA

Haleakalā National Park

HALEAKALĀ
CRATER

KAUPŌ

NI

Science City

KULA

ʻUlupalakua Ranch

WAILEA

MĀKENA

Watercolor map by Pamela Hayes

Photo Credits